W0114046

DESIGN IN A FRAME OF EMOTION

by **HANNAH BEACHLER** with **JACQUELINE STEWART** and **TONI L. GRIFFIN**

————October 4, 2018
Piper Auditorium, Gund Hall,
Harvard University
Graduate School of Design

————Supported by the Rouse Visiting Artist Fund————
Produced by Ken Stewart, Paige K. Johnston, Patric Verrone
————Published by the Harvard University
Graduate School of Design and Sternberg Press

TONI L. GRIFFIN: Welcome to tonight's Rouse Visiting Artist Lecture. I am delighted and fangirl-geeked-out to welcome Hannah Beachler and Jacqueline Stewart.

AUDIENCE: [*Applause*]

TONI: This conversation, about filmmaking, placemaking, and—a new term I just learned—world-building, will engage both the imaginary and the real, intersecting with the work that we do here at the Harvard University Graduate School of Design. ——— World-building is the process of constructing the imaginary. It requires many of the same considerations for the production designer that we consider as architects, landscape architects, urban designers, and planners: What's the geography and the ecology of place? What is its culture and its political and/or development history? Who inhabits these places? What are their practices and traditions? How do they seek and find shelter, food, social interaction? Where do its citizens gather, convene, and create community? What shapes the image of the city? What values or aspirations do we hold for its city dwellers? What utopian or dystopian terrain best enables the society's tale to be told? And what is the dominant cultural normative? Is it masculine or is it feminine? Is it Blackness? Is it whiteness? Is it nationalists or is it nonconformists? We share these considerations in the work we do as designers. ———— In the United States, city-building from whole cloth is virtually nonexistent, or at least limited to the ways we build new suburban or exurban developments. However, globally, rapid urbanization trends are constructing new geographies for work, dwelling, commerce, entertainment, and social services. For our design professions here at the GSD, city-building most often responds to existing context, including politics or political leadership, economics and regulatory constraints, and socioeconomic patterns. And our interventions are often constrained by these contexts. ———— World-building, on the other hand, is free from these constraints and can construct both the desired and the fantastic. World-building constructs a city for the purpose of its inhabitants

THE INCIDENTS

to play out specific scenarios of either conflict or celebration, solitude or community, in their most idealized forms. The intent of world-building can be daring and even confrontational, or it can be functional, practical, or accessible. Place-setting, either through world-building or the reimagination of existing places and spaces, is an integral part of the storytelling process of filmmaking. Place as context can be background or foreground, political or agnostic, compliant or complicit, real or imaginary, masculine or feminine, Black or white. ———— I am excited and curious to hear what Hannah and Jacqueline can offer us as example through their creative process and examination of the role of film and the city, and I hope that we might learn from their methodologies new approaches to understand and practice space-making in the built world.

———— Hannah Beachler is a prolific production designer who crafts unique emotional landscapes for every story. She recently began preparing for her next project with director and frequent collaborator Melina Matsoukas on the pilot for FX's *Y: The Last Man*, a television show based on the comic book series. She designed Marvel's *Black Panther* for director Ryan Coogler, which just became the ninth-

highest-grossing film of all time—
like, all time.

AUDIENCE: [*Laughter, applause*]

TONI: Her incredible work
earned her a 2018 Saturn Award for
Best Production Design. She previously collaborated with Ryan on
Creed, starring Michael B. Jordan
and Sylvester Stallone, and *Fruitvale
Station*, which won the Prix de
L'Avenir in the Un Certain Regard
competition at the 2013 Cannes Film
Festival. ——— Hannah also collaborated with director Barry Jenkins
on the 2017 Best Picture, *Moonlight*,
a coming-of-age tale that transcends
traditional genre boundaries. In 2016,
Beachler designed Beyoncé's stunning
visual concept album *Lemonade*—

AUDIENCE: [*Applause, cheers*]

TONI: I see the Beyhive is in
the house. We'll get into that. For
Lemonade, Hannah took home the
2017 Art Directors Guild Award
for Excellence in Production Design
for Awards or Special Events, and it
also earned her a 2016 Emmy nomination for Outstanding Production
Design for a Variety Nonfiction Event
or Award Special. ——— Hannah will

be in conversation with Jacqueline Stewart, a professor in the Department of Cinema and Media Studies at the University of Chicago. And tomorrow, Jacqueline will be inducted into the Academy of Arts and Sciences.

AUDIENCE: [*Applause*]

TONI: Jacqueline's research and teaching explore African American film cultures from the origins of the medium to the present, as well as the archiving and preservation of moving images and orphan media histories, including nontheatrical, amateur, and activist film and video. She directs the South Side Home Movie Project and the Cinema 53 screening and discussion series. Jacqueline is also director of the Gray Center for Arts and Inquiry at the University of Chicago, and cocurator of the L.A. Rebellion Preservation Project at the UCLA Film and Television Archive. She serves as an appointee to the National Film Preservation Board. Jacqueline is author of the book *Migrating to the Movies*: *Cinema and Black Urban Modernity*, which has achieved recognition from the Society of Cinema and Media Studies and the Black Caucus of the American Library Association. —— Ladies, the floor is all yours. Thank you and welcome.

JACQUELINE STEWART:
It's such a pleasure to be here with you. Hannah has selected a range of images that are going to be running throughout our conversation, and we're going to try to keep up with them. ———
Can I ask a super basic question? It would be great to know what a production designer does. What do you oversee? Where do you enter into a production?

HANNAH BEACHLER: I come in pretty quickly. I get a script, usually in development, a little before preproduction. I'll read it, and if I decide I want to work on it, I'll meet with the director. I'll put together a presentation, or a deck, to show how I understand the script visually and how I connect to the story.

I consider myself more of a story designer than a production designer. When you go to see a movie, it's because you want to laugh, or cry, or you laugh through your tears, or you get angry, or you get a sense of inspiration, and everything you see and experience on the screen is contributing to these feelings. People don't often recognize the production design, which encompasses building and designing the sets, set decoration, and props, as well as costume design, hair, and makeup. It's all the texture you see on-screen that moves you toward one emotion or another in complement with the story. ——— Sometimes I manage a lot of people. But on something like *Moonlight*, I wasn't overseeing anything—it was a crew of five women. We did everything. For such a small-budget film you really have to be resourceful. Decisions happen on the fly because there isn't a lot of time in the schedule. You don't have a lot of time to shoot. As the production designer I also go with the location manager to find locations that fit within the frame of what we're doing. And then I'll go with the director and say: *Look at these things. This is what we could do here.* Or: *This is how*

we can augment it here. I have to keep in mind the camera and blocking, and add details that you won't even see on film. All those things are in consideration when I design an individual set. —— Then I consider the crew. For instance, there has to be more than one entrance on set, depending on the size of the film and things like the complexity of its crew and sound stage. There can't be a bunch of people coming in and out of a single door. I have to find hidden ways to integrate doors into the design for those purposes.

JACQUELINE: You play an incredible translator role when you speak to the larger vision of the film. And at the same time you have to manage so many logistics, like where people can come and go, or where the camera can be placed in a particular scene.

THE INCIDENTS

HANNAH: I also have to consider the weight of the crane, which is 5,000 pounds and six feet wide—which I know now.

AUDIENCE: [*Laughter*]

HANNAH: For a period piece like *Miles Ahead*, I wanted to go into old places and old homes. What you just saw as the boxing ring was in a very old cathedral that was converted into an event space. And as soon as you walk onto it, you know the joists in the floor are no good and it has a sublevel for the cellar. If you bring a crane in there, it'll go right through the floor. So you have to get an engineer to come and tell us how much weight we can put on the floor, and then we have someone shore it up. I'm thinking about all of those logistics as well.

JACQUELINE: I imagine you have to pull together a wide range of images. In *Creed*, you had to think about the franchise and what the previous *Rocky* films looked like. If you're going to take up the life of Miles Davis, there's a lot of complicated, interesting, and sometimes conflicting information about him and his space.

HANNAH: That's part of the design within *Miles Ahead*. By the time we get to him, he's 75 and he's addicted to heroin. We're not really sure where he is. Miles couldn't really remember anything because of the years of substance abuse. His life was so big and he was so big that everything got squished together into one big moment. ——— A lot of what you see is from different periods of his life all in one place and time, because he can't put it together. So, when he's telling a story about the jazz club, he could mean Birdland, or he could mean

THE INCIDENTS

a jazz club in Paris—he could mean anywhere. We tried to put those things together when we did the Village Vanguard. We made the interior of the jazz club the color of the Village Vanguard during the time he played there, but we made the exterior in the color and design of Birdland. And when we see the story about him being arrested, the jazz club in the film is designed to represent the fact that he can't remember which club he was at when he was arrested. It was about his memory, and his inability to think beyond or outside of himself. That's what we wanted to do.

> JACQUELINE: There's an amazing scene in that film. He's in an elevator, and then a wall gives way and he's in a nightclub. There are so many ways you were playing with set design to get at this sense of his jumbled memory. —— It seems like you must have a lot of fun shopping.

HANNAH: You know, everyone says that—when you come up to the cashier with five carts, and you're sweating, and your phone is ringing, and everything is going off at the same time, they'll ask: *What job do you do? That must be so much fun.* And you think: *Does it look like fun right now? Because I've got to get to the car, I've got a meeting in five minutes.* I don't shop much anymore, except to select from whatever the set decorator brings. But when I was a set decorator—I tried to do every job in the art department—I did a lot of shopping, and that made me the fastest shopper you'll ever be around. I learned store layouts, and I usually already know what I want and where to go when I get there. I don't have time to waste.

JACQUELINE: OK, I said "shopping," but maybe we should call it "curating"?

HANNAH: *Curating*, that's what I do now.

JACQUELINE: You're selecting things with an eye toward what's going to work together in the right combination at a precise moment. —— I'm thinking about that in relation to *Lemonade*.

HANNAH: *Lemonade*! The queen.

JACQUELINE: The term *curation* comes to mind because this seems like a really complicated text. There are multiple directors. It's not a single narrative that moves across different sets.

HANNAH: And I only got to hear one song.

JACQUELINE: Is that right?

HANNAH: Yeah, I laugh about that now, but it wasn't funny at the time. I thought: *Really?*

AUDIENCE: [*Laughter*]

HANNAH: One song. I think it was "All Night." ——— It was a lot of switching gears. You want to show a deconstruction of a woman's feelings in a relationship that she's trying to hold on to, or fix, or heal, and then do that healing within herself and gain strength, because first, you're mad, then you want to kill everybody. Then, it's like: *OK, can we work this out?* ——— We needed to break that down while bringing in the aspect of Black empowerment for Black women, which I think is a very different thing from just Black empowerment. Female Black empowerment is different because Black women are oftentimes overlooked and not heard, especially in this country—well, that's always the case, but we're particularly feeling it now, and she wanted to get that out there as part of the design: a place where you can feel small at times and you can

THE INCIDENTS

feel powerful at times, but by using the canvas of 18th- and 19th-century plantation life. In that sense, *Lemonade* was a bit Afrofuturist. We took the reality of the plantation in New Orleans, which was a place of great oppression, especially for women—a place of rape and utter dehumanization—and turn it on its head by making it a place of empowerment, a place of education and alchemy. The scene in the brick kitchen is our interpretation of the women learning about apothecary. ——— You see these women at the dinner table. You see them in the dining room. You see them inside. You see the matriarchs and older women. We mixed the idea of very traditional, colonial construction with African textures. We took Victorian chairs and covered them in mud cloth and wax cloth and things of that nature to create a sort of mix of the two, the oppressor and the oppressed—and the juxtaposition of the two, reconcilia-tion. ——— It was all about this deconstruction, so there was no one thing I needed to do as a designer, because there was no real formal structure. A lot of what I do is very nuanced in terms of story or world architecture. My father was an

THE INCIDENTS

architect. My mother was an interior designer. I've been around it my whole life. My father's process was always very oriented in the build, in the material, and in the land. ——— I always speak of design in a frame of emotion and less the "hammer and nail" of it.

> JACQUELINE: It makes perfect sense why you would be the one to do *Lemonade*, which is all about exteriorizing this internal emotional landscape in so many different forms, and bringing questions of race, gender, and class into that.

HANNAH: Absolutely, and class is a big one. I had to make it really feel like every "set" was the deconstruction of an emotional moment in this woman's life—so you see the parking garage in "Don't Hurt Yourself," you see the plantation in "Sorry," you see the porch in "Forward," you see

the little girl running out the front in "Interlude," and you see the paper stage in "Freedom," which was inspired by old Victorian toy paper stages for very wealthy children—like paper dolls, but they were houses, and stages, and they were beautifully painted. So I had that stage hand-painted as well. It's reclaiming something.

JACQUELINE: You just touched on something that seems really important in your practice: what's visible and what's not visible. Things that the audience never sees. There are elements you add to your sets to motivate actors, giving them a sense of the space and ideas for inhabiting their characters—and you do it just for their sake, not necessarily to be seen by the audience. Could you share some of those kinds of details?

HANNAH: I do that all the time. It's so important for performances, and for actors to believe they're in the world you created. In *Black Panther*, there was a lot of back-and-forth: *Do we use effects? Do we build? Do we use effects? Do we build?* It was very important to Ryan [Coogler] and me that we built, because we needed to create a tangible world. It wasn't going to work otherwise. And you could see the actors touching the sets and interacting with them. They go through a discovery as well. ——— Oftentimes, I'll get feedback from actors who are like: *Oh, that's there. OK. I didn't know that about my character. That really helped me connect to my character.* Take Tessa Thompson's apartment in *Creed*. Her character Bianca had a lot of knickknacks and little things around her place. I called Tessa's assistant and said: *Send me some of her things.*

JACQUELINE: Her personal things?

THE INCIDENTS

HANNAH: Her personal things. She has a tattoo that says *yes* on her wrist, and that's a big thing for her that goes deeper than just the word. We had this *yes* on little things in her apartment, and her knickknacks were around too. When she walked in, she was blown away by it. —— I worked with Tessa a lot on her space. We added all of the music—mixed DVDs or CDs—she would have made as a musician. The weekend before we started shooting, Ryan, Michael [B. Jordan], Tessa, and Ludwig [Göransson], the music supervisor, spent the weekend in that apartment just hanging out and chillin', playing music, vibing, getting to know her space—what she would be doing if she lived in Philly as a musician at that time. Ryan was like: *It felt like she lived here forever.* And that's the goal.

JACQUELINE: So, *Black Panther.* —— I was in the grocery store the other day, and a woman was like: *I love your haircut. Did you get that after Wakanda?*

JACQUELINE: She didn't say the name of the movie, she didn't say the name of any actress in the movie. She just said: *Wakanda*. Wakanda is invoked as this incredibly profound idea for lots of people. Did you have any idea of the role you would play in creating this sense of Wakanda—which was not a new fictional thing, but now has this life that is astounding? Are you surprised by the resonance it has had?

HANNAH: I was absolutely surprised. My expectations are always really high. But for this, because it was my first time with such a huge movie, my whole bar was like: *Just, please, people, go. Go to it, and then don't kill me in the critique of it.* It's one of those moments when you look back at your life and

THE INCIDENTS

think: *That was really courageous of me to do that*. At the time, you probably didn't feel courageous at all. ——— I didn't think it was going to be more than what I've done on any other film. And I didn't necessarily feel that—not until after the movie came out. Then I'd get on Twitter and I'd see videos of people dancing in lobbies and dressed up—and not celebrating just African heritage, but anybody's heritage, whether that be Asian, European, Latino, or anything else. People were dressing up in their ancestral clothing and celebrating who they are and where they came from, and I'd be crying every day, and I'd call Ryan saying: *Do you believe this?* And he's like: *I can't speak. I don't even know.* We all thought: *We've got to hide. This is crazy.* We didn't expect anyone to react in this way. ——— For all intents and purposes, Ryan, Rachel [Morrison], and I should never have been there—or would have never been there had we not had people believe in us, and who could actually pull the trigger to get us on a film with the size and presence of *Black Panther*. Kevin Feige, Victoria Alonso, Louis D'Esposito—they're the ones who got us there. We, in that sense, had something to prove. I know I did. For Rachel and me, as females—especially for me as a Black female and the first Black female to design a superhero movie— we had something to prove. I went in thinking: *All right, I might die at the end of this, but I just gotta go at a thousand percent for 14 months.* And I did. We were on multiple continents. We had stages in Atlanta and we were doing R & D in Los Angeles; we were shooting in Busan; we shot second unit in South Africa and second unit in London. I had teams in all of those locations. I went to each place once for initial scouting, but then the teams went over and did the work. I did not go back during principal photography. It was always like: *What time is it where you are now? It doesn't matter, just tell me what's going on.*

JACQUELINE: A huge range of topographies had to be created for this. In the interest of thinking about some questions about urbanism—how you were thinking about cityscapes, urban architecture, urban space, and transportation systems—what were some of your guiding principles in the way that you and the whole creative team imagined what this center of Wakanda would look like?

HANNAH: Ryan really was our guiding light through all of this. I grew up on a farm, so I was not brought up in a city. With him being from Oakland, the Town and the City, he has a real sense of being in a city both as a young person and as an adult. He really wanted Golden City to feel dense in its skyline. When you see the big cityscape, we wanted it to feel like there are a lot of skyscrapers and high-rises and that

THE INCIDENTS

the city is really packed. Then, there's another feeling when you're on the ground. ——— What I brought to it was a lot of thought and research about the continent of Africa, and all of its countries. One piece of research I did was a study of the different climates on the continent. How did the tribes and the different peoples in different countries deal with those climates and environments? What I found was that historically a lot of Africa was about migrating. In the 3rd to 7th centuries BCE people weren't migrating so much because they were fleeing some war or horror, but because of the rainy season and the dry season. Tribes would go downstream during the rainy season, and rebuild their entire village that was just wiped out by flooding upstream. It became tradition for some tribes. It also had to do with economics, for example: *OK, we can catch more fish during these months because we're going to be flooded out upriver.* And then there's all the rebuilding. You don't see many records of precolonial villages because they would, in large part, be wiped out, destroyed, and at times lost. When colonialism started in the 15th century, most tribes

THE INCIDENTS

stopped migrating. It was a matter of migrating for economics and preservation of community. And then Europeans came in and said: *OK, now you're trapped. We're creating borders.* There weren't really borders before in sub-Saharan Africa. There were different tribal areas. And when they started establishing borders, oftentimes two warring tribes would be in the same area, or two friendly tribes would end up separated. The whole economics of those tribal lands then changed.

—————— Because Wakanda wasn't colonized, we wanted to show that migration still happens to a degree within its borders. The epicenter of that migration is Golden City. In essence it's like an Oakland, or a San Francisco, or a New York, where you have many people from the different tribes in Wakanda move to "The City." We looked at it as a very metropolitan city. That's why you get the mash-up. It reflects back on African American culture and experience. As an African American, I innately brought some of my culture to *Black Panther.* When I'm sitting next to you or any Black person, we're from different places, but we're not. —————— It's not necessarily about just

THE INCIDENTS

the city or the diaspora. It's about the way people lived before colonization. That's what we wanted to show, and then add the modernity of progress on top of that layer. I had to build the topography of the country before I could start deciding: *Where is Golden City in this country? And why is it there?* You'd say: *Because it's where the palace is located. The palace would be someplace that couldn't be traversed. You shouldn't be able to cross a border to get to it, so you needed to surround it with mountains.* That's why there are all the steps and tiered land— which was a big part of agriculture in sub-Saharan Africa, and something that was wiped out during colonization. Tiered land was the best way for water to feed land without having the technology to do it. ——— I had to think about Golden City 10,000 years ago. They were farming on tiered land, which is still there because the Golden Tribe were farmers and they were the first people to settle in Golden City. The next tribe who came was the Merchant Tribe. I took and adapted the history of the Meatpacking District in New York City, which was created by Native Americans for trade and selling goods:

the underground cooling brine systems in New York were why the vendors only sold things at night. You don't really see it on-screen, but Merchant District is only open at night, and it evolved over time into a more residential and nightlife place. So its story evolves in the same direction as the Meatpacking District. The Merchant Tribe then realized they can sell their goods to other tribes who were now in the area, and coming into the city. ——— And I completely made it up. I'm telling a story that isn't true. I just realized I'm going on like this is some real thing, and I absolutely made up the fact that Golden City even exists.

> JACQUELINE: But it's incredible that you can fool yourself with your story.

HANNAH: I totally fooled myself. As though I am actually telling you real, factual continent-of-Africa stuff. And it is not. The Merchant Tribe isn't a real thing. But that's how deep we had to go. I had to understand why Step Town existed.

———— After the Golden Tribe became the royal family and was no longer farming, the tiered land started to develop. That's where we have Step Town. That's why it's called "Steps." It's also called "Step Town" because it's where young artists come to gain experience. When you see Step Town, you see a lot of Afropunk-looking people. You have the lip plate, and you have Ndebele painting on one of the buildings. You have some Senegalese artwork. You have the braai cooking on the street. And then you have the hoverbus going by. These young artists take their tribal traditions and evolve them into a new art form, a new tradition. The other traditions are still there. That's not denied. That's not destroyed. It's still a part of the community. Those spaces then become open spaces, physically and spiritually.

> JACQUELINE: You're helping us understand how layered your thinking, your research, and the actual visual design has to be in order to give that sense. You're answering the

question of why the idea of Wakanda
resonates with people so strongly.
——— Because it's not completely
disconnected. Although you could
call it a fantasy space, there's so much
about it that's tied to the actual,
historical, cultural, economic histories
you guys have been tracing.

HANNAH: Absolutely. It's about community. It's about
family. It's about kids. It's about rituals, spirituality, the things
that you don't see in normal futurescapes. Futurescapes tend
to be overpopulated, with too many buildings, and they can't
all fit. It's the film *Elysium* where all the rich people live in a
perfect society in the sky, while the earth is this overpopulated
cesspool where humans have robotic body parts attached in an
effort to enhance them physically or prolong their lives, and
they work and produce for those in the sky. It's these horrible
futures that we think: *That will never bleed back into our*

THE INCIDENTS

reality. It's just entertainment, and it's fun. But it actually does bleed back into our reality.

> JACQUELINE: Where are Black people in the future?

HANNAH: There aren't any. I don't know how many aliens with elephant heads there are, but you will be hard-pressed to find more than one Black person in a *Star Wars* movie. I think there were two Asian women in the last one. But how many camels with body parts are there? I'm looking at this, like: *He's a lobster, but you can't have more than one Black person?* OK, come on now. It's not a hopeful future. What do you have to look forward to? How do people then look around their own world filled with all kinds of people—maybe not in some communities, but the world is generally diverse—and then reconcile that in film the future is only filled with people of European descent, and that's it? What's the point? So now, it's time to put something different on screen.

THE INCIDENTS

You put Black excellence on screen.

AUDIENCE: [*Applause*]

HANNAH: In many different ways. To put tradition back in the fold. To evolve something and not just plunk it down because it looked cool. To take a tradition and say: *OK, how did that serve them through time? And what are we seeing of it now?* ——— We made a timeline for Wakanda that started in the Bronze Age, and it went to the present day. This timeline covered where we were, and all the points we hit in the real Western world. Then I thought: *OK, now let's all sit down and figure out what Wakanda was doing. When did they have the Internet superhighway? What were we doing?* We were still figuring out how to get the Pony Express to California, and they had the Internet. We had to figure out why they hadn't been hacked yet. *It's because they don't work on a binary system. They have a completely different computer system. So we can't hack it. They can hack us, because they can mimic a binary system. But we don't know yet what their system is.* ——— I know what it is, but you don't know.

JACQUELINE: We're going to have Professor Griffin come up and join us.

TONI: I'm completely fascinated by this constructed development history you're walking us through, which is related to economic and social trends and how the city responds around it. ——— In the United States, Black narratives are very much tied to land. You've now constructed a whole narrative for this place, Wakanda, that some people really believe, and some people are kind of annoyed that people believe it. Your consideration of Wakanda includes references to places we know from many different contexts, and some imagined spatial elements. ——— I have a two-part question. I want to get Jacqueline's response to this, as she's looked through a catalog of Black film, and it's about the way in which she's seen the city show up as a vehicle for telling the narratives of Black Americans. We have a lot of Black films that try to tell Black stories within white spaces, and not within a uniquely constructed space. Hannah, you've been able to deconstruct that in *Lemonade*. It was deconstructed in Childish Gambino's video as well. So, I would first like you to talk about how effective Black storytelling and Black film has been used in the United States context to enable that story. And then I want to come back to Wakanda and ask you about constructing such a richly developed history. Who were your collaborators in building that story?

——— In listening to your remarks this evening, I now understand you more as a story designer than a production designer. As such, you have historians, architects, landscape architects, and ecologists as part of your story-building team. How do other disciplines inform the way you create these histories and then ultimately create the environments that you do?

JACQUELINE: The figure of the city across African American cinema has always been prominent. And the city has been a problematic space—I think for the most part it has been represented as a space to which people have attached great hopes, and those hopes have been dashed. ——— We can take this all the way back to the early race movies that were made for segregated audiences in the 1920s, 1930s, and 1940s. People go to the city and that's where you become corrupt. That's where women lose their every-thing. That's where families fall apart. We can trace this through the Black independent cinema of the 1960s and 1970s. I'm thinking about the L.A. Rebellion Group, for example: Haile Gerima, Charles Burnett. The city is a space of tremendous difficulty and oppression. People are subject to the city, and the struggle is how to find agency, how to navigate the space in a way that makes you feel as though you can be a whole person and keep Black community intact. We see that through the *Boyz n the Hood* films of the 1990s—the police state, economic exploitation. I love the reel you shared with us. And especially my favorite line in that film: "Don't scare me like that, Colonizer!" I think the historical processes of colonizing and decolonizing help us understand what you and your colleagues are doing. It has to do with decolonizing the cinematic imagination and centering Blackness. —— In *Moonlight*, which you could see is a story of a kind of abjectness, there's actually a different relationship between Black people and urban spaces that suggests there can be intimacy or some kind of human connection.

TONI: So it's a manipulation of context. You have to take the Miami out of Miami in order for the Black narrative to be told, and for us not to be distracted by the glamorized Miami that exists in many of our imaginations. You've created a constructed space by manipulating a real place.

HANNAH: You see Little traverse this urban concrete jungle. If you go out to some suburbs, you see they've taken the concrete landscape and repurposed it into skate parks and other new spaces. If you go into urban areas, which are not funded by the state equally, everything is crumbled. ———— Little is running from these kids because of who he is. He runs through this landscape, past the trouble and the drug dealers who are there to make money, and he hides in a "trap" house. Once inside he sees all the destruction, the human destruction of self. He sees the needle for mainlining, and the spoon, and the garbage, and then Juan takes that board off the window and this light, *pssh!*, comes through—I'm a big sound maker— and illuminates him. This is Juan, the person who is going to illuminate him within this construct of what some would call an urban nightmare.

TONI: Is the yellow we see through *Moonlight* supposed to remind us of the illuminating of Juan?

HANNAH: Yes, definitely. The yellow, and the blue of the car he's in. That's him. The water—it's that lightness. It's when you look up at the sky and you think of the universe, or God, or whatever you think of when you look up—that thing that's so much bigger than you. To Little, that's what and who he was. When that light came through, it could have been an angel. It could have been God to him. ———— When Juan brings Little into his home for the first time, the home is a soft pastel pink. Because that was Miami—the teal and the pink. That's very Miami without being *Birdcage*.

TONI: One of my favorite images from this evening was the plan of Wakanda, annotated with districts, the Center City, the university. It was fantastic. —— I would love to unpack your process a little bit more. I know you immerse yourself in your own research and with the rest of the filmmaking team, but do you look outside of your discipline to build that body of research, particularly for such a richly developed place that does not exist? Tell us about who you collaborate with, and how your collaboration process works.

HANNAH: We collaborate with a lot of people. We brought in a couple of architects who are working on designing a Google City. This is a completely technological city. They shared how they plan to make it more of a communal residence with shared yards. All transportation is underground. All the technology is behind walls. There's a shared currency. They're basically building this city so you would never have to leave. Everything you need is there. —— They're telling me this, and I'm soaking it in because I want to understand what someone like Google thinks the future should look like. I said: *Who lives here? Because what you're describing, I can't even afford it. So who's living here?* All of a sudden, I see the big circle in the sky and Matt Damon, like: *I'm coming.*

AUDIENCE: [*Laughter*]

HANNAH: Clearly you'd have to have money to live there. That's not useful to me. So mute on that. Because then, I don't want your idea. I don't want to be inspired by something that's only for a few. Thank you for the information, but it's not the information I'm looking for here. ——— We did bring in geology experts to talk about vibranium, the strongest metal in the world, which is the metal that Cap's shield is made of. I had to become an expert in metallurgy at one point because I had to know how one would mine something as powerful as vibranium without exploding all of Wakanda—or the earth, for that matter. How does that much vibranium enter the atmosphere? We also had to talk to a lot of biologists and nanotechnologists especially in regards to Black Panther's suit. ——— And a big part of this was my dad's voice—the architect, the perfectionist, saying: *You need to know what the land looks like, Hannah, before you can build anything.* He would always say that to me. I'd be like: *Draw me a house.* And he'd say: *I don't know what the land looks like. I can't draw you a house.*

AUDIENCE: [*Laughter*]

HANNAH: I don't know if that's a lazy thing. I'll have to talk to some architects here. Was he just messing with me? Did he just not want to draw me a house? Or is that real? But I took it as real, whether it was or wasn't. I realized I needed to understand the land.

> TONI: I'm excited to go back and watch the movie again after hearing you describe the importance of land as a narrative. I want to now examine where the city's development history—through architecture, through density patterns—may be different in different scenes of the film.

———— Anytime we move through an urban environment, we can tell the history of the city by what is no longer there, what remains, and what is new. We can then begin to overlay the socioeconomic story and histories that remain or have been erased, to complete the story of the place. I'm curious to go back and look at the landscapes you've created to figure out if I can trace the story you've told us through what we see. For example, I wonder if I'd be able to distinguish richer neighborhoods from poorer ones. ————
I read an interesting article critiquing the film for not showing poverty. The article went on to say: *Well, why would you want to see poverty in Wakanda? It's Wakanda.* There was a debate about what society should be like, and how the built environment represents those forms to society, so I'm curious to look for that. ———— I also have a handful of African friends who are architects. When *Black Panther* first came out, I was like: *It was so great! Aren't you excited?* They're like: *Eh.* Not because they didn't like it, but they were very conflicted by the mash-up— the way in which the many different cultures of Africa, a continent of many distinct countries, seemed to be seamlessly mished and mashed and swirling around, and they were really

challenged by that. My interpretation of their concern was, because most of the world is quite frankly not very well informed about the continent—its culture, what's progressive, what's metropolitan, what's rural, and its history overall—that Wakanda was creating a false narrative, and now people are going to think Africa is like this and still not understand the texture and complexity of the continent. I'd say: *Well, let's put that on the table and use the art to introduce and expand awareness and education.* And I think you've done that tonight by explaining your constructed historical narrative.

——— There is a conviction you have to have as the designer, the person visioning something, to withstand critique—to withstand it as a Black woman leading that vision. All these forces come at you, and not just on this film, but probably every film and in every aspect of your life. There are 115,000 architects in this country, and just under 500 are Black women. I'm sure the same demographics exist in your field as well. ——— Tell our students about what it took for you to hold true to your vision for Wakanda and all the other films you've created. How do you show up in defending your vision?

THE INCIDENTS

HANNAH: I stand by what I do. I always say, when I'm working with my crew: *I'll fall on my sword. I'll fall on my sword for you. I'm not falling on anybody else's sword.* That's all I can do. I'm a failure if I don't learn from criticism. I'm not a failure because something didn't work; I'm a failure because I didn't learn from it. ——— If the concern is that we don't know enough about the continent, and then people see Wakanda and think they do, I'd honestly rather them misconstrue it that way than what I grew up with for 48 years. I would rather have a child sit in a classroom and hear: *Well, in Wakanda, it's awesome*, instead of them mispronouncing the country of Niger, and be the only Black person in the room at age seven. That's painful for a kid. ——— I think, for me, that's the big difference between African and African American. I don't see myself being either one. I place myself in the space between. That's where I am right now. This view is my perspective as a little Black girl who grew up in a predominantly white community in the countryside of rural Ohio, and how I felt when people said things to me about Africa—all the hurtful, derogatory things that you hear as a kid. *All Africans are uncivilized.* I mean, our president basically called Africa and many developing nations a shithole. ——— Wakanda creates a new kind of narrative, because it was created from love, from hope, from joy, and from what our future can be and may have been.

> TONI: You said: *This is my vision as a little Black girl. This is how I want people to see it.* All three of us are each little Black girls from segregated cities in the Midwest. Maybe I can expand my curiosity about Black space by asking each of you to talk about how the female perspective or

the feminine city shows up in your work. How does the feminine story show up? Jacqueline, you've been examining a wide breadth of Black films. Is there such thing as a feminine city? How do you see it show up in your work?

JACQUELINE: One thing we talked about with *Lemonade*—"we" being Black feminist media scholars— were the resonances between it and Julie Dash's work, especially her film *Daughters of the Dust*. It's not set in an urban environment, but it's about the prospect of going to the city and what you try to hold on to before going.
——— Hannah, across your work, I can see a lot of resonance with the kinds of questions Black feminism has been addressing for a long time about making space, about creating a sense of community, about honoring the intimate and recognizing how the personal impacts our ability to do political work. I see you firmly in that line of thinkers and activists. We normally focus on directors when we look at film authorship. But we should focus more on film artists like you working behind the camera. This may be a small number of women of color, but you are incredibly powerful, creative, important women who do work that

sustains the same kind of feminist viewpoint over time. ——— I have a project in which I collect home movies shot by people on the South Side of Chicago. Mostly by dads and uncles. But the home movies that are shot by women are doing exactly what you do. They pay attention to the food and to the child's play and to home decor in different ways.

TONI: The settings that enable life to take place versus the setting as a coincidental backdrop.

HANNAH: It's exactly that. I was very lucky on *Panther*— specifically working with Ryan, whom I consider a feminist. He has a sense of intimacy and a sense of place within an interior: the detail to the children, to the family. That's always very important to him. ——— Yes, there's a sense of Black feminism. As a Black woman, I always have to be in this position [*sits up in chair*] when I work: always "on." I've got to be forward. I have to be up. I have to be shouldering every-thing at all times. As a Black woman in this industry, you can't ever do this [*slouches in chair*], because the minute you do, you're seen as weak, vulnerable, not useful.

TONI: Or you recede. You become invisible.

HANNAH: Yes, exactly. And in that weakness you're able to be controlled. I'm a Leo, so that's just not a thing. But you do find yourself getting weak of constantly doing this, of constantly being strong. It's exhausting. ——— It's in my work: a sense of constant female strength. Especially with Black women. With *Lemonade*, of course, I was with Beyoncé. The queen. I worked with her again in Jamaica just recently for all the interludes in *OTR II*. It was a little more nurturing, and it was a little more sexy. We did a lot of stuff with dance-hall, and it was about Black women being able to own that femininity of being sexy and not just childbearing, over-wrought, or all the other tropes that we're presented with at any given moment, on any given day. But to be soft and feminine, vulnerable, and emotionally exposed, because you don't really get to be those things as a Black woman. Sometimes I do just want to be vulnerable. Sometimes I don't want to be the one who has to take care of everything. ———— I try to create that in the spaces where there's a strong sense of women, like in the throne room in *Black Panther*. We talked about things like: *There's going to be all these king's guards-men and council of elders in the space. Where does everybody stand?* Well, they stand on the top level of the throne room, looking over the council and anyone coming and going. The women stand on top. The king's guard are down on the main level and off to the sides, and the women are on the top level, where there are giant 10-foot sigils made of clay and mud behind the Dora Milaje representing their tribes. It's the matriarch.

> TONI: So now everybody should go back and watch the film through a feminine lens this weekend.

HANNAH: I am telling you, somebody is going to come after me from Marvel and be like: *What are you saying about these things?* Well, I never changed it. Have a fabulous laugh about it.

TONI: We have time for questions.

AUDIENCE: Jacqueline, I want to go back to your comment about decolonizing the cinematic imagination. Could you talk about how your scholarship looks at that?

JACQUELINE: One way I try to address that issue is by looking at spectatorship—Black spectatorship. As much as I'm interested in what filmmakers do and what's put on the screen, I think a key part of what happens in cinema is in the exchange. There's so much that happens at the point of reception. There's a loop in which meaning is being constructed. —— This is one of the reasons *Black Panther* is such an important film. You alluded to this—the fact that people were turning out dressed Wakandan. I did an outdoor screening of *Black Panther* this summer, and we had a costume contest. I thought it would be maybe two or three people. Nah.

TONI: It was the entire audience.

JACQUELINE: Everybody. Think of the ways in which African Americans have figured out how to find pleasure, even with films that were not designed to provide any kind of entrée for us at all, sometimes just finding those small moments to connect. To be able to appreciate what a maid is doing in a classic Hollywood film, or to somehow make the narrative work for their own purposes, I think is tremendously creative. That's a really important way I can see a kind of decolonizing happen in relation to whatever the text might be originating.

AUDIENCE: Hannah, when you talked about transforming the *Lemonade* production set from a place of oppression to a place of empowerment, why did you choose to think about that transformation versus creating a whole new landscape?

HANNAH: When the artist tells you what they want to do, you have to figure out a way to do it. It was important for her to be on that plantation. It was important for her to take that ownership back. ——— It could have been an entirely new place. But it would have become something different. The feeling of what she was trying to convey is not new, but how she handles that feeling is new. That's how we learn. That's how we evolve. We're faced with the same stuff over and over and over and over and over again. It's how we decide to handle it each and every time. If we do the same thing every time, then we're probably insane. But if we learn, we can do it a different way. And that's where I think she was coming from. I wanted to create a freethinking place. We shot a lot that you didn't see, where the women who lived on the plantation were learning to shoot guns. They were learning archery. And then they all had duties in the kitchen. A lot of that was edited out. But I think you still got the feeling with the women in the garden. —— She's very smart about that. She knows herself well enough to know that she's had that feeling before. And this is how she's going to take charge of that and take power of it.

AUDIENCE: I have a question about the insertion of the humanity of people of color, both in the histories you constructed and the resulting features. Particularly with *Lemonade*. I feel like when we talk about planta- tions, we often ignore the slaves. They're just kind of background people, and their humanity's not there. But you inserted women of color there and created this powered ethno-future. And in Wakanda, we often think of Africa as a colonized or untamed place, but you inserted humanity and history. —— How do you do that? Because in general, with futurists and media, we don't see humanity in people of color in the past or in the future.

HANNAH: Well, I do it because I'm Black.

AUDIENCE: [*Laughter*]

HANNAH: And I'm human. So I put those two things together. —— In *Lemonade*, having Black people at the front was a very important thing. That was part of a taking back. In a way, that felt more useful than some of the language that we used to say we're taking back. It was about the matriarchy and not the patriarchy. It was about generations of women and what we see from generation to generation in *Lemonade*. —— We placed Wakanda—a fictional, African nation— above Burundi. We kind of fudged it and scooched it closer to the DRC and we moved Lake Kivu down a little because we wanted it to be on the border of the Impenetrable Forest. No big deal, right? We just moved some stuff. After we placed it there, I looked at the surrounding countries of who would have migrated to this one little spot 10,000 years ago. And it's mostly sub-Saharan. —— When we see Africa, it's either Tarzan or Egypt. In Egypt, the dark-skinned people are the bad people or the slaves. If it's Tarzan, it's the help—Black people are the help. So again, I think Wakanda is just another form of destroying a narrative—or giving humanity. Like Oscar Grant in *Fruitvale Station*. I'm going to give him his humanity. He's a son and a father. Because then, you can't look away. You can't just walk out of the theater like whatever. You have to think about it a little more. It's more present. And you think: *Oh, OK, these are people.*

AUDIENCE: I see a lot of depictions of Africa that—as somebody who is African and grew up in Africa—are totally alien to me. I cannot relate to them. There are fictions out there anyway about Africa that are different from the reality of it. ——— But I love this fiction. It's something we can have a conversation about, and it's inspiring.

HANNAH: Thank you. When I was in South Africa I realized nothing can replicate what you see with your eyes when you're there. So we weren't trying to do that. We weren't trying to replicate the vastness and the beauty on camera. We can only capture an essence and the feeling I had—a sense of joy, a sense of pride in your tribe. A lot of Xhosa people were our guides and they talked to us about the Afrikan history, about colonization, about Apartheid, and what that did to the farmers in the land grab. ——— I knew I'd never be able to fit thousands of languages and thousands of tribes and cultures from this ginormous place. It's huge. That's not a possibility. And had I tried to do that, it would have been an absolute failure. I needed to capture all the things I saw: women walking down the street wearing great, colorful skirts with colorful socks that came all the way up, and the way they held babies with a cloth wrapped around, their little legs peeping out. You just wanted to grab them and kiss them. And the smiles and the joy. Watching kids in a township playing soccer. They'd kick it over the edge and have an argument about who would go to get it. All of that. Watching little kids dance, eating the food. I could only do so much to capture the smell, and the texture, and the essence of everything I saw there. I was never going to re-create it.

JACQUELINE: It's not about all fiction being bad, nor does your research have to be so exhaustive that you get every particular detail right and include it all. It seems like there are lessons there and implications for design. If you think of Wakanda more as a kind of design fiction where you play out different possibilities, rather than something that's accurately documenting or trying to be true to a variety of relevant disciplines, then that honors the creative work you're doing. That can then animate all of the work we try to do in all of our "real world" disciplines.

HANNAH: It speaks a little to gentrification and migration. Are they supposed to give up the way they know to build? The way they know to create and craft? Because now all of a sudden there are two other tribes around them? It's like: *Oh, well, we're not going to do that anymore. We're going to create something completely new out of it.* No. Part of that is allowing a space for you in your culture and your tradition.

TONI: And how does the creation of that space evolve as other migrants and other histories disrupt it? As an essence informs your work, a set of values also informs your work. I always ask my students and clients, what are the values we think we're bringing to design—and not just, what is the spatial, technocratic approach?

THE INCIDENTS

I want to know how values translate into design and respond to the context.

AUDIENCE: How were indigenous African religions and their spirituality present in your concept of designing the film?

HANNAH: A lot of that spirituality was surrounded in the City of the Dead. We had to come up with how the vibranium was discovered in the first place, and we went toward a religious and spiritual direction, that it was discovered by the monks. That inspiration came to me from the film *Samsara*. *Samsara* is fabulous. Vibranium is sensitive to energy and sounds, so when our Wakandan monk started a meditation with a low, almost baritone vocalization—similar to some African traditions—they noticed the vibranium was becoming brighter and heating up. ——— A lot of African tribes bury the dead. But in Wakanda, they both bury and burn the dead. One way they burn the dead is by laying vibranium rocks around the deceased, and then gather around in a circle. They would do a low vocalization, and the vibranium reacts to the vibrations from the vocalization, that then heats up the rocks and burns the body. That's how they found fire in Wakanda, tens of thousands of years before any Western nation. Through that spirituality and through their religion, they advanced themselves. Unfortunately, that didn't end up on the screen. ——— But maybe in *Black Panther 2*.

AUDIENCE: [*Laughter, applause*]

THE INCIDENTS

Image Credits

PP. 12–15   Stills from *Moonlight*, directed by
                      Barry Jenkins (New York: A24, 2016).
                      Credit: A24/Photofest.

PP. 16, 19   Concept sketches for *Miles Ahead*,
                      directed by Don Cheadle (New
                      York: Sony Pictures Classics, 2015).
                      Courtesy of Hannah Beachler.

PP. 17–18, 20   Stills from *Miles Ahead*. Credit: Sony
                      Pictures Classics/Photofest.

PP. 21–28   Stills from *Lemonade*, visual album,
                      directed by Beyoncé Knowles-Carter,
                      Kahlil Joseph, Dikayl Rimmasch,
                      Todd Tourso, Jonas Åkerlund, Melina
                      Matsoukas, and Mark Romanek
                      (Parkwood Entertainment, 2016).
                      Credit: HBO.

PP. 30–31, 34–41   Concept art for *Black Panther*, directed
                      by Ryan Coogler (Burbank, CA: Walt
                      Disney Studios Motion Pictures, 2018).
                      Courtesy of Hannah Beachler and
                      Marvel Studios.

PP. 32–33   Still from *Black Panther*. Credit:
                      Walt Disney Studios Motion Pictures/
                      Photofest.

Contributors

HANNAH BEACHLER is a prolific production designer who crafts unique emotional landscapes for every story she designs. She made history as the first African American to be nominated for an Academy Award in Production Design, which she won in 2019 for her work on Marvel's *Black Panther* (2018), directed by her frequent collaborator Ryan Coogler. She previously worked with Coogler on *Creed* (2015) and *Fruitvale Station* (2013), and with the director Barry Jenkins on the 2017 Academy Award winner for Best Picture, *Moonlight* (2016). She also worked on visuals for Beyoncé's 2018 OTR II tour, as well as on her visual concept album *Lemonade* (2016), which earned Beachler the 2017 Art Directors Guild Award for Excellence in Production Design and a 2016 Emmy nomination for Outstanding Production Design.

JACQUELINE STEWART is professor in the Department of Cinema and Media Studies at the University of Chicago, and directs the South Side Home Movie Project and the Cinema 53 screening and discussion series. She is also director of Arts + Public Life at the University of Chicago and the host of Silent Sunday Nights on Turner Classic Movies.

TONI L. GRIFFIN is Professor in Practice of Urban Planning at the Harvard University Graduate School of Design, director of the Just City Lab, and founder of urbanAC, an urban planning and design practice in New York City. She has developed comprehensive plans for Detroit, St. Louis, Milwaukee, Newark, and Washington, DC. She has also published several articles and book chapters on the just city, legacy cities, and urban planning and design, and has lectured extensively in the United States, Europe, South Africa, and South America. In 2016, President Barack Obama appointed Griffin to the U.S. Commission of Fine Arts.

Acknowledgments

The Harvard University Graduate School of Design extends
its gratitude to the collaborators who make the Incidents series
possible, especially Meg Sandberg and Matt Smith, as well
as the Building Services team and Securitas personnel at Gund
Hall, without whom events at the GSD would not happen.
Special thanks to Kahlil Joseph for his help in making the
event with Hannah, Jacqueline, and Toni a reality.

On the occasion of this series redesign, special thanks to
Jennifer Sigler and Leah Whitman-Salkin, who edited the first
seven volumes of the Incidents, and to Åbäke, who designed
them. Thanks also to Shantel Blakely, Paige K. Johnston, Patric
Verrone, Lindsey Grant LaGrasse, and Pamela Larsen, who
organized the public programs depicted in those volumes.

Colophon

Design in a Frame of Emotion
Hannah Beachler with Jacqueline Stewart and Toni L. Griffin

Published by the Harvard University Graduate School of Design
and Sternberg Press

Designed by ELLA
Edited by Marielle Suba
Proofreading by Barbara Darko
Printed and bound by Grafiche Veneziane
Distributed by The MIT Press, Art Data,
and Les presses du réel

ISBN 978-3-95679-559-6

© 2020 by the President and Fellows of Harvard College and
Sternberg Press. All rights reserved. No part of this book may
be reproduced in any form without prior written permission
from the Harvard University Graduate School of Design.

Harvard University
Graduate School of Design
48 Quincy Street
Cambridge, MA 02138
gsd.harvard.edu

Sternberg Press
Caroline Schneider
Karl-Marx-Allee 78
D-10243 Berlin
sternberg-press.com